The Common Song

Poems by
Eva Maxwell

Many Voices Press
Flathead Valley Community College

My heartfelt thanks to Lowell Jaeger, Hannah Bissell, Margene Berry, Meliss Clark, Neal Brown, Nancy McLain, and my husband, Max Maxwell, who spent hours editing my poetry as well as his own.

Front Cover: Watercolor painting of Wetz house on Watson Road, Clinton Township, DeKalb County, Illinois. Image copyright ©2020 Eva Maxwell.

Back Cover: Eva in Glacier Park—Photo from the Maxwell family album.

Text Layout by Hannah Bissell

Many Voices Press is a non-profit press from Flathead Valley Community College. Donations are tax-deductible. We depend on the generosity of people like you. For more information on our books, please contact:

Lowell Jaeger and Hannah Bissell, Editors
Many Voices Press
Flathead Valley Community College
777 Grandview Drive
Kalispell, Montana 59901

Phone: (406) 756-3907
Web Address: manyvoicespressmt.com
Email: ljaeger@fvcc.edu

Softbound ISBN— 978-1-7336918-3-3

Cataloging-in-Publication data on file at the Library of Congress.

Library of Congress Control Number: 2021900466

Created, produced, and designed in the United States.
Printed in the United States.

The Common Song

Time held me green and dying
Though I sang in my chains like the sea.

—from "Fern Hill" by Dylan Thomas

Poems by Eva Maxwell

Dedicated to my Grandma

Mabel Westlake Mundy

1879 – 1967

Table of Contents

Midwestern Young

yes

A Day with You, My Seven-Year-Old Self

It was a Winnie-the-Pooh sort of day,
soft blue sky, puffy clouds. You and I

went for a walk along the byway
to Howison's Woods, a mile or two.

You were young, maybe seven I'd say,
and already biting your fingernails,

standoffish, shy, but at ease when I told
you tales of robins, foxtails, old elm trees.

We popped joint-grass, gathered wild roses,
blew milkweed fluff out of pods in the breeze,

stamped on mud curls, skipped and ran until
I, no longer a girl, was out of air.

Back at the farm, you climbed a pear tree.
We put doll clothes on baby kittens,

ate brown sugar sandwiches, gummy bears too,
and sang all the silly songs we knew.

Then, still humming, we squeezed into one chair
and read stories of Piglet and Pooh.

Aging alone, I am child within crone,
reliving sweet days with you.

Country School Field Trip

Each of us carried a brown paper bag.
Teacher led the way. I walked with my best friend,
a third-grader named Alice. We scuffed our way
across the Somonauk Creek bridge. To our left
was the old-fashioned farm, the tidy fields
worked with horses, tall and gray.

We were on our way to Howison's Woods
to gather hickory nuts and golden leaves.
As we turned off the gravel into the dark grove,
I walked a little closer to my older friend.

Maple and elm, I had thought I knew trees.
But hickory trees were eerie Shaggy Men,
strips of bark hanging from their lofty trunks.

The ground was covered with the pale nuts.
We filled our bags like winter-hungry squirrels,
like dwarves who had struck a windfall of gold.

I was wide-eyed, enchanted,
that such a magical forest stood
so near my home, less than two miles away.

At age six, I thought I had things all figured out.

Hay Mow (Rhymes with Cow)

Cathy and I ride up on our bikes.
We call from the road, a Wild Indian whoop.
Yes, Phyllis is there, coming out the back door, waving.
We race up the lane, an eye on barking, biting Tippy.

Up the ladder to the stacked bales
piled to the roof on the far end of the loft.
Climbing, scouting to find the perfect spot.

Three girls tugging bales this way and that
to make a fort (beware of thistles).
Camouflage so the boys can't see it,
in case they come looking for us
(which they never do).

Rest cross-legged in our stronghold,
breathe the grassy air,
watch the dust dance in the sunlight.

Hear Lady wuffle in her stall below,
shifting her long-legged weight.

Lean back, picking thistles
from the palms of our hands
and the soles of our sandaled feet.

Let slide in the drowsy air,
    worries about the biting dog,
    our mother wondering where we are,
    that first big step backward onto the ladder
    when we go down.

Thanksgiving Dinner Tensions

Gathered together for dinner the four of us,
plus three grandparents and our young aunt,
around the table set with flowered china
and the etched tumblers with silver rims,
footed serving bowls heaped with mashed potatoes,
turkey stuffing, sweet yams and more.

Grandma Mundy sat, ready to eat,
her polite face shiny from kitchen heat.

But first, we must have a picture.
Aunt Ruth, Dad's youngest sister, snapped the shot,
her mother, my Grandma Wetz, smiling fondly.
Perhaps there had been a little quip,
a jest about making everyone wait,
a doting mother-daughter chatter.

Dad at the head of the table, arms crossed,
looking without warmth at the camera.

My dark-haired mom, not turning to face
the lens, the corners of her mouth tightened.
Is she annoyed at the foolish joking
between her husband's mother and sister?
Is she merely impatient at the delay?
For Heaven's sakes, let's eat; it's getting cold.

Little dark-eyed Cathy lifting her round face,
curious, like the Grandma beside her.

And I, hunched forward in my chair, eyes narrowed,
knowing that something was going on
besides dinner.

First Dance

Last day of school
third grade picnic
at the roller rink

laced shoe skates
ease onto floor
open windows catch breezes

music like carousel
strides lengthen
faster, faster

skirt swirling
a white swan
lifting off pond

flying, beautiful,
transformed
by the phrase, the beat,

and made whole.

Who We Aren't Is
Who We Are

At my new school
a third grade game
there were no rules

two teams
running and screaming
for no clear reason

in bushes
on ball fields
behind buildings

when the Others
came flying around
a corner of the school

we screamed and ran
the game seemed serious
we were spies

or cops or robbers
it was who we were
I didn't know why.

Fifth grade
two teams
boys, girls

boys chased us
holding a big turtle
we ran and screamed

I still didn't know why
I wasn't afraid of turtles
but I knew I was a girl
so I ran.

Everyone Needed a Bath

The climbing roses, rich and red,
twined around the post of the old porch,
their fragrance both sweet and cloying,
stealing my breath in the humid air.

Trying not to sweat and spoil my bath
of a few minutes before,
I twirled and spun and spread my arms,
my skirt stirring a welcome breeze.

I could hear Dad calling Mom to come
scrub his back. Dressed to go, his
sandy hair, usually standing straight up,
was combed into respectability.

Mom had washed her dark hair into soft waves
around her face. We girls had slept uneasily
on metal curlers the night before.

Earlier in the day, Grandma treated
herself to an old-fashioned sponge bath,
flannel wash cloth, soapy water,
clouds of Spring Bouquet talcum powder.

A lemon jello cheesecake waited
in the Philco. It would be perfect
with the ham salad sandwiches
that were an after-the-meeting favorite.

The monthly Grange meeting was bucolic
ceremony, lifelong family friendships,
and a night for us country kids to run
wild down the streets and alleys
of our sleeping town,

chasing each other into a future
we could not have imagined.

Grandma Teaches Embroidery

Yes, that is a good design. Not too hard.
Do the leaves first in a green outline stitch.

Cut off a length of floss, then take three strands
in each hand and pull to separate.

Thread the needle now. Watch me, I'll show you.
Touch the strands to your tongue to make them one.

Here, I'll do it. You make everything so hard.
Now tie a knot. Loop the thread and pull.

Your knot is too big, too lumpy, not neat.
Well all right, that will have to do. Now

let me show you. You have to hold the thread
just right, be consistent, not too tight.

Pay attention now to what you do.
Uneven stitches on your green stem.
See how it's puckered? Better undo.

All right. Next we must change to pink floss for the roses.
Did you tie off your green? I doubt that will hold.

What do you mean, you're getting shaky?
Embroidery's easy. Better than crocheting
for you.

Now, let's see the back. Yes, the back.
Good embroidery looks as good on the back as on the front.

Now where are you going?

Come back here!

After a Piano Recital: Eight Birds in a Tree

When the hollyhocks bloomed in front
of our teacher's house, we knew it was time
to get serious about piano.

On the night of the too-soon recital,
the parents crowded into the lace-curtained
parlor. We girls sat with sweaty hands
in the dining room, waiting to play,
wearing Easter dresses and shiny shoes.

No written programs, we announced our pieces,
mispronouncing titles and composers,
then launched into our new-learned music.

I don't remember what I played the year
I was ten years old, or how it went,
except that it was somehow good enough.

What I do remember is,
after the last piece was played, we grabbed
a few cookies and headed outdoors
to run while inside our parents drank tea.

And in those fancy dresses, slippery shoes,
we climbed the apple tree beside the gate,
then sat silly on the branches and laughed.

Not a Carnival Kid

I waited for her a long time in front
of the horticulture building. *Mom says*
I can't play with you any more, she said
when she finally arrived at our meeting place.

We had so much fun that morning,
roaming the fairgrounds, ducking into tents
to get free stuff like pencils and combs,
laughing at pigs and goats in the animal barns.

My Mom and Dad operated our honey stand
from morning till late at night for five whole days,
selling honey, summer's work extracted and bottled.

Checking out the rides was my opening day ritual.
I liked the Flying Scooters best. I watched
the big kids and saw how they veered the planes
on their chains toward the center post then swooped
way out over the heads of bystanders.

I tried a few "Prize Every Time" games,
won a carnival glass cup for my mom
that, as an eight year old, I didn't really want.

I put nickels into a vending machine
offering black and white portraits of movie stars
for me to study in my ongoing concern about my looks.

After while, after my money ran low,
I got tired of running around by myself
so when I met Judy, just my age, I was glad.

Why not, I asked, *why doesn't she want you*
to play with me?
She says you are a carnival kid.
I knew what she meant— I'd seen their rumpled clothes
their super-dark tans from sunny days spent running the rides.

I'm a regular kid, I said. *I'm really smart*
at school, and I know how to tap dance, I said.
We live near here and just sell honey, I said.
I told her that, said Judy sadly.

She walked away and after a bit so did I.
To mend my hurt, I slipped into the Church Tent,
inspected the shiny crosses on chains
then signed up for a mail-in Bible course.

Grumpy Love

My grandma and I got along best
on those summer evenings when side by side
we cooked fried cucumbers for supper.

Sliced lengthwise, salted to get the bitterness
out, allowed to weep on the counter,
dipped in egg and cracker crumbs,
fried golden brown, served with sweet corn.

As a rule I shunned cooking, cleaning,
and needlework. Grandma was accomplished
at the household arts and my lack of perfection
in them seemed to make her peevish.

She looked at me with a face of judgment:
too big, too clumsy, uncooperative,
lazy, careless. *A big lummox*, she said.

I looked at her with scornful eyes:
too fat, too picky, too forgetful,
smelly, just too old.

And there was the issue of five people
in a two-bedroom house. Until I was
twelve years old, I slept with Grandma
in the little bedroom off the kitchen.

I saw her old underwear, her tired
pajamas, her urgent bathroom rushes,
heard her breath puff out as she
fell asleep, leaving me wide awake.

You will be sorry when I am gone,
she said, her voice grouchy as usual.
I held my scowl, but a pang in my heart
told me she was right.

You don't know what's good
she sniffed as I turned up my nose
at something she had cooked, like
mustard pickles or fried cornmeal mush.

Now it's me, old, slow, hopelessly inept
at things like computer games. *Grandma, no!*
our granddaughter shouted at age four
as I tried to rescue her princess.

It's me, rushing to the bathroom,
complaining about my back, falling
asleep in my chair, forgetting friends' names.
I begin to understand what aging can do.

And also it's me, knowing now that love
was transformed with a treadle sewing machine,
into a blue and yellow quilt for my room,
my very own room without my grandma.
I pray that I thanked her for that,

and for all the cooking and baking,
weeding and hoeing, scrubbing and
dusting, she offered us in her eighth decade,
manifestations of her grumpy love.

Take-Home Pay

A September evening at the Fair
brought a cool breeze, a hint of fall.
The crowd emerged from the grandstand show.
Car-jumping daredevils,

dancing Rockettes, guitar playing cowboys
headed for their trailers as small children
were carried toward the parking lot
in their dads' strong arms.

The midway suddenly crowded, engines
that powered Ferris Wheel, Octopus, Tilt-a-Whirl
roared beneath the screams of kids,
and waltzes of Merry-Go-Round.

Young couples strolled hand in hand,
he throwing hard-earned cash at the chance
to win a Teddy Bear for her to take home,
to prove their love.

Years later these same couples stopped
at the stand near the junction
where Fair met parking lot to pick up a pail
of honey for morning pancakes.

Take home a little honey, your wife won't mind
urged the sign painted on the trailer.
Jars of honey lined the white shelves,
small to large, comb, chunk, back-lit to glow.

The beekeeper and his wife stood inside
chatting with neighbors, selling the sweet goods
from the shelves behind them. I was often
there too, with my nose to the glass

of the observation hive, pointing out the queen,
longer, darker, with her ladies-in-waiting
circling her like petals around a sunflower.
Do you get bit much? people asked.

Bees don't bite, they sting, I scowled,
exhausted from a day of eating
Pronto Pups, cotton candy, going
on the rides, helping Dad and Mom.

But I always perked up when we got home,
heaps of cash to sort and stack.
Sweet gold given us by those zealous workers
who threatened us with stings all summer long.

She Taught Us to Play

Mom, intrigued by her style, chose Irene
Grandgeorge to be our piano teacher.
Mom had seen Will and Irene out dancing,
black skirt flaring as they dipped and turned,
and had heard Irene entertain, smiling
sweetly to the audience as she nailed
a tricky running passage.

A hasty presentation
of the basics, then off we went.
Book after book of light classics, 1940s pop,
hymns, duets, opera transcriptions.

She said to me once, *Your sister can't do that*,
after my poetic attempt to play
Debussy's expressive harmonies.
My little sister could play fast songs by ear,
earning much family glory, but Mrs. G heard
and honored my own musical gift.

She sang along as we played,
laughed with us at our mistakes,
hugged us before we left
for another week of practice.

She offered me the joy of
"playing" the piano.
The work could come later.

Secrets

For my tenth birthday, an airplane ride
above the countryside,
a quilt of black, gold and green velvet squares,

a gods-eye view of the land below,
many mysteries lurked unseen.

A grid of clay tiles, laid beneath the land
draining spring thaw and summer rains.

Hidden in fields, grotesque, fungal corn smut,
In the woods, mushrooms and tree roots.
in underground communion.

Where was the secret nest of sticks that
        hatched the great blue heron?
How did his yellow eye spot
        the flooding, the insects and rodents
        in a small corner of the cornfield?

And the stories:
Tales of the Underground Railroad
that sheltered runaway slaves, so near
our house, on the old Chicago Road.

The untold story of the five Olson girls,
who somehow lost their parents, and were
adopted by locals, but known as sisters
by their identical blue eyes.

And my Grandma, already gray
when she came to live with us,
her braid of rich brown hair in her trunk,
with a silk shawl and a Victorian card
from a man named Frank
that we never knew.

Too Hot to Sleep: DeKalb County Illinois

I move my pillow to the foot of the bed,
a wisp of air curling through the open window.
Leaves whisper in the darkened maple,
answered by the deeper rustle of corn,
the shaky call of the screech owl in the orchard.

The evening's last lightning bugs rise, blinking forlornly.
Beyond them, a star holds me, tranquil and steady.
The breeze freshens, the curtain lifts.
I inhale deeply.

A car turns off the highway onto the gravel road.
I know the driver has his windows down, cooling air on his face.
There is a comforting companionship in the crescendo of sound.
A passing whoosh and a spray of gravel leave me alone again.

The Trapper's Vision

Thirty pelts of muskrat, beaver, and mink
nailed meticulously to the wall
behind my jaunty grinning dad.

A teenager with home-made fur hat
carelessly upturned coat collar, wool
baggy pants, hatchet hanging from belt,
rubber work boots.

A farm-boy mountain man
who didn't take it kindly
when someone robbed his trap-line
in the creek that ran along the edge
of the family farm.

Standing in the dark farmhouse kitchen
near his mother's wood stove,
he told her of the empty traps.

In the telling, in his mind's eye,
a vision of a burning footprint,
a boot track so detailed, so clear
he could match it the next day with a particular
pair of boots in the school coatroom.

Quietly, casually, he divulged to his friends
including the owner of those guilty boots,
he had set a bear trap to catch the thief.

He chuckled as he told us the story.
The truth is there was no bear trap,
no money to buy one,
but, the pilfering did stop.

What was that vision?
The glowing boot track of justice?
Or just an unregistered memory?

Dad and Mom Play Cards with Lloyd and Grace and I Learn a Thing or Two

The men shouted, guffawed, pounded the table,
playing cards as partners, against their wives,
bidding with confidence and glee,
each urging his cohort to raise the bid,
holding only the ace and queen of trump between them,
not knowing who had the right and left bower,
who the king . . .

perhaps it was the wives, faces impassive,
steady brown eyes meeting partner's tired green,
quietly taking tricks while the men
groaned and bemoaned their ill fortune.

Grandma and I awake
in our room nearby, smiled
as Mom played the joker.

We just didn't have the cards, Dad said.

We'll catch up to 'em this time, Lloyd boasted.

Dad lit his cigarette, shuffled, and began to deal.

To an Old Love

I liked you the first day I came to you,
your solid frame, your dark good looks.
As a first-grader from a small country school,
I was swept away by your dignity.
You smelled of furniture polish,
paper, ink, and glue.

Sunshine through your west windows
warmed the children's reading tables.
Peeking out, I saw our little town,
businesses along the highway,
depot, bandstand and village clock.
You stood at the bend where US 30
veered left before roaring toward Chicago.

You were such a story-teller,
I couldn't resist you. We started
with Dick and Jane and ended
twelve years later, sharing
Gone with the Wind and Dostoevsky.
I was so completely smitten with you
that I wanted to read every book on your shelves,
but the limit of four per week
held me in check.

I visited you last summer but you were
not open. I stood by the door at the top
of the stairs, looking toward town,
missing the large oak tree that once stood
between you and the highway.

I heard a rustling behind me
of those long-ago leaves. *Or was*
it the footfalls of our storied friends
walking lightly down the steps?

The Bobbsey twins holding Raggedy Ann,
Mole and Ratty with Jimmy Skunk and Reddy Fox,
Nancy Drew arm in arm with Cherry Ames,
followed by the Hardy Boys, Tom Sawyer,
Topsy, Jo March, and Johnny Tremain.

Down toward the street they seemed to go
and into my car, parked at the curb,
where they waited to go home with me,
as they always had.

White Gloves

Minnie Mouse, skinny black-clad arms
ending in oversized white gloves.
Always dolled-up, always a star.

Why did little girls have to wear clumsy
white gloves to church? Hats with stiff fake flowers?
Ill-fitting sweaty nylon dresses?

Their grandmothers shopped department stores,
viewed fine gloves in narrow boxes,
studying fabric and seam, fit and price.

A girl might wish to tap-dance in black tights
and leotard, a top hat, striped shirt,
sparkly white gloves to catch the lights,

lift the spirits of the willing crowd,
clicks and stamps streaming from her shiny shoes,
white gloves winging above for grace.

She Walked

A reticent girl, she dreamed
of becoming a nun and living
in a cathedral monastery,
probably in France.

She would wear a simple habit,
no worries about fashion, hair-dos,
or boyfriends, and would walk
quietly, humbly in the corridors
near the wall, praying.

Her church had no monasteries, so she prayed,
sang and learned to play the pipe organ.
Overwhelmed by her family, she trod
the gravel road between clover
pastures and fields of corn,
red-winged blackbirds as confidants.

Eccentric?

Wetz is eccentric, I overheard
in the crowded cafe. I sidled past,
hoping no one would recognize
this daughter who didn't know whether
to be ashamed or proud.

He did, I admit, build curious things . . .
a steam bicycle powered by corn cobs,
smoke, even flames, rising
from the stack behind him
as he coasted down the lane,
pipe between his teeth.

And he did talk, and talk . . .
fearless speculation on
impending ice ages, flying saucers,
polar shifts, hypocausts,
plains Indians, boiler controls,
the genius of cats, especially his cats.

His sky blue eyes blazed as he warmed
to his topic. Sparks flew from his pipe.
His sandy hair stood on end. A friend maintained,
John Wetz is the smartest guy I ever knew.
He might have agreed, with a sheepish grin.

He wasn't interested in pearly gates
or streets of gold, he said. If he wanted
to play the harp, he would do it now.
Sounds boring, he said, apologizing,
on that afternoon eight years ago.

I imagine him today,
curiosity too big to die,
cruising the universe,
searching,
inquiring,
speculating. . . .

Back to the Land

Mr. and Mrs. Cook taught art in the City.
Sometimes enduring gray windy winters,
they imagined how it would be to
summer in the country, living quiet,
natural, unfettered in the sun.

And so one spring they bought a rough
piece of land along Little Rock Creek,
built a cabin. One room, a loft,
kerosene lamps, wood stove, a pump organ
for hymns and old-time music.

Their second summer, they met Mr. Wetz,
local beekeeper, and were pleased
by his proposal to move forty swarms
of bees to the creek in exchange
for their fill of natural, organic honey.

The third summer, the Wetz family was asked
to a harvest dinner. Meadow greens
added a bitter weedy flavor to the salad,
tough field corn from a neighbor's back forty,
was boiled starchy, inedible.

After dinner, a lamplit glow renewed
the smiling faces as they sang with
the crickets long into the evening,
accompanied on the pump organ
by the buxom Mrs. Cook.

Perhaps it was in the fourth summer,
Mr. and Mrs. Wetz drove to Little Rock
to tend the bees. She waited in the truck
while he stopped in to say hello. The cabin
door stood open, the room was empty.

He walked around the corner of the house
and there, in a lawn chair, in the sunshine,
was the rosy nude Venus, Mrs. Cook,
au naturel, eyes closed, long wild hair
let down, a look of bliss on her face.

Mr. Wetz whirled around and walked quickly,
quietly back to the pickup,
slid onto the seat, chuckling, red faced.
You'll never guess what I just saw, he said
to his wife, easing the truck into gear,

ready, so ready to get out of there,
to find safe ground to work the bees.

The World Comes to Me

Even then at nine years old I knew I did not want
to live in Clinton Township all my life
and that led me somehow into stamp collecting.
Leafing through my album I saw

Woman tapping a rubber tree in Ceylon
Women gathering crops in the Philippines
Man shooting an arrow at the sky in Guyana
Men in loincloths hollowing a canoe in Togo

Leopards, camels, gazelles
elephants with scimitar tusks

Saints bearing crosses above cathedrals
Explorers and their sailing schooners
Asian royalty, palm trees, waterfalls

I ordered big grab-bags of stamps,
and spent hours sorting them, putting them
into my book, counting them, savoring
their foreignness, my ticket to the world.

I saw the stories of nations' change.
King George, then daughter Elizabeth
were scattered through the Empire's colonies.

Hatchet-faced Hitler was profiled
on the stamps of German-occupied nations.
A black border paid tribute
to a war-dead Hungarian aviator.

Free China, led by Chiang Kai Shek,
his picture displaced by Chairman Mao,
beside the same sampans and ancient Great Wall.

Sri Lanka was Ceylon back then.
Thailand was Siam.
African colonies later became nations
like Zaire and Zimbabwe.

Would you be willing to have a roommate
from Africa? the Dean of Students asked.

I'd been dreaming of Africa all my life.
Now Africa was coming to me.
I said *yes. Definitely yes*.

Honey

If you have seen the bee yards nestled
in shady groves or near fallow creek banks,
If you have seen bees flying home
single-mindedly from the fields
of sweet clover and purple alfalfa,
If you have seen jars of golden honey
at the DeKalb County fair,
you may have known of my family's wealth.

We were rich in beeswax, dripping with honey,
on pancakes, sandwiches, cereal,
in apple pie, cookies and lemonade,
even on tomatoes and grapefruit.

Our colds were nursed not by store drugs,
but with lemon and honey for sore throat,
honey taffy for a cough.

Extracting the sweet riches from the hives
was late summer's work. After
uncapping, whirling, clarifying, straining,
my parents filled industrial-size tanks
with the colonies' summer savings.

The outraged victims of this thievery buzzed
around the honey shed,
around the pickup,
around the back door.

Door knobs were sticky
Steering wheels,
even fingers, all sticky,
the smell of honey cloying
in the thick muggy air.

Good Intentions

She had flown into the pickup cab
as we were on our way home
after working bees all afternoon,
in one of Dad's many bee yards

She buzzed up and down the windshield,
nose to the glass, with an occasional
wild sweep past our brows.

As she started exploring the side window,
I rolled it down and watched
as she was flung out into the summer day.

You didn't do that bee any favors,
my dad said quietly.
I hadn't wanted him to crush her,
to pinch her thoughtlessly before she could sting
as I had seen him do so many times before.
I had thought saving that one little life
would somehow make a difference.

Did she die right away
from the force of the wind current?
Did she find herself alone beside the road,
too many miles from her hive?

Despite my good intentions,
all I could do was
offer a silent apology.

Fireflies

In autumn I again visited
the lake, the surface softest blue.
Bands of mist or coastal smoke hid the
exact point where water met land,
where water met the sunlight sparkling
like silver fireflies rising

as they did evenings from the tall
grass at the edge of the cornfield when
he and I were midwestern young.

We caught them gently, imprisoning them
in mason jars with holes nail-punched
so they could breathe and blades of grass
so they could eat

to collect them for a lantern
to light some dark night wandering

but of course they got away.

For Chopin's Ballade

I've been seeing you every day for two years.
You don't notice our anniversaries, but I do,
my life is so entwined with yours. From the beginning,
I knew that we would have a special connection.
Together we've explored every nuance of feeling,
the most intimate details.
You've shown me the depths of your soul.

Now the day is coming, too soon. I'm not really ready,
though I do have the dress, the shoes I'll wear.
What if I am too nervous, too shaky to go through with it?
What if I let you down; they all sit there, unmoved, coughing?
Our fate is in my ten unruly fingers, my easily distracted mind,
my overwrought emotions.

Soon it will be over. My friends will be kind, bring me flowers.
You will be mine, my special piece of music for a while,
until someone else meets you, falls in love.

Why?

I Play Piano

for the same reasons the birds sing
on spring mornings, to be noticed,
to be chosen for love. Yes, but more
for the joy of singing,

for the same reason that toddlers yell
watch me Mom as they speed down the slide,
because my parents admired music making
and I hoped piano would make them admire me,

for those times my emotions flared too strong
during storms, after quarrels, better than slamming
doors, a meditation that cooled
angry words,

for the thrill of surviving a musical skydive,
stepping onto the concert stage in a sparkling gown
with a head full of harmonies
and a heart full of butterflies,

because the world is so far from faultless
and I can't fix it, but I can take time
each day to cultivate an oasis
of something enduring and true,

because not playing
brings me a peculiar uneasiness,
brings a shift in the universe that reduces
a shooting star to a small, plain rock.

Clink of Spoon, Clatter of Knife

It was the clink of spoon against cup,
mixing canned milk with perked coffee,

the clatter of cheap knives and forks
against plates of hot breakfast,

the smells of coffee, of bacon,
rising to the upstairs room, where I lay,
not yet ready to come downstairs where

my dad sits reading the paper to my mom,
one foot up on the chair to ease his back,
she in her pink robe, half-smiling
at news reports that confirmed her hunch
the world was absurd,

the kitchen window open, humid breezes
trading Dad's cigarette smoke for bird song.

Far from that home for many years
I still now and again hear
the clatter of silver on plate,
clink of spoon in cup
and just for a moment,
I am home with Mom and Dad.

Home Ground

After I left, the house became a graying shell
Grandma died, the orchard died,
the flowers wilted. Mother, tired
of scrubbing, let the dirt build up
on the holiday china. Dad sold the house
and within a few short years, it burned
to the ground.

Did the old toad who lived in the damp
corner of the cellar survive the fire?
Did the flames kill the peonies,
the bridal-wreath, the roses? Is the
once-white barn still standing, the green sign
HONEY nailed to its western wall?
The embers of memory still glow within me.

I drove there last summer, several years after the fire,
finally ready to accept what I would see.

The road is still narrow gravel past that empty homesite,
red-winged blackbirds still call in the evening.
The breeze rustles the leaves of the corn pressing close
to the deserted place like an ever encroaching woods.

I must tell you how it began . . .

The man, the woman bearing the child,
the new-divorced grandma, pooled their money.
Two bedrooms, water from a cistern,
shade trees, an apple orchard
on two acres surrounded by fields of corn.

Cold, drafty, the bungalow was warmed
by good food. music of piano, harmonica
and the man's stories of small engines,
of guys at work and of his bee yards.
To check the facts, he kept the encyclopedias
within reach on the shelf by the table.

The woman and her mother gardened,
cooked, canned, cleaned black Illinois dirt
from floors, furniture, clothes, children,
taught the girls to mind their manners,
do their homework.

How safe I felt, sitting idly
in the swing, under the arching elms
humming and waiting for the time
when I could leave this home behind me.

Out West

A Job Out West

It was early afternoon
of the fourth day that I arrived
in my new hometown,

dustier, shabbier
than I remembered
from my interview in May.
The wind was gusting
paper and debris
down the main street.

Everything I cared about
was packed into my
red VW Bug. Books,
piano scores and LPs,
teaching attire and the new
stereo that my dad
bought me after my
boyfriend break-up.

Each state had merged into the next
as I headed west.
My little car pushed on,
uphill and into the wind.

I sang song after song as I drove,
making up the words I didn't know,
gave rousing sermons
on civil rights and social equity.
I had never been so completely
alone for so long.

Then Montana. Sweeping mountain
ranges scattered at random.
Room to breathe under the wide sky.
Dusty, empty, entirely new.

We, my car and I, were a tiny ladybug
crawling along the rough highway.

I could see far into the future.

First Fall in Havre

Two blanket Indians passed me
on the dusty sidewalk,
that autumn afternoon.

Blond scalp, the words I heard
quiet, but distinct.

A thump of heart,
A sidelong glance.
Graying hair in braids,
worn blankets pulled tight
around their shoulders
against the wind.
Faces impassive,

but for a flicker
in the dark eyes.

We passed, went our ways,
they, pleased to have
teased this white girl,

I, pleased that I got the joke.

yw

Hop In

Shall we tell the kids how we met?
Tell them that you were starting down
the runway at the Missoula airport

in a Cessna one-fifty, when you saw me
standing beside the tarmac, the wind
whipping my thin skirt around my legs,

my blond hair around my incredible
face, and that you circled around, landed
and took off again with me on board?

No? Try this. I was spinning out of
control down the Clark Fork River
in an inner tube, a self conscious

mermaid in a new swim suit.
When I saw you, a wiry curly-haired
savior on the far bank, I called

help me. You plunged into your
canoe, paddled gallantly,
ardently, nudging me ashore.

Or tell them my friend and I were waiting
at the light on Higgins Avenue
and you came rolling by in your

lovingly-polished lipstick-red
convertible, gliding to a stop.
Here he is, my friend proclaimed
and you said, warm and friendly,

Hop in. So I did.

If I Hadn't Married into a Ranching Family

I wouldn't have known
  these big men in work coats,
in from morning chores,
  stomping the snow
from their boots,
  faces glowing from the cold
under scotch plaid caps,
  glasses fogging in the
steamy kitchen,

  sunlight bright
on the breakfast table.

Kitten Love

If I were a little cat,
I'd luxuriate upon your lap.

You would stroke my downy fur,
I'd close my eyes and start my purr

and vow to keep my sharp new claws
hidden in my velvet paws.

Puppy Love

If you were a chubby pug,
you could snooze upon the rug

beside my old piano bench.
In your dream we'd jump the fence,

run and dream-bark all night long,
singing the piano's song.

Saving the World One Load at a Time

She pulls the machine, rotund, four short
legs, into the middle of the basement
floor, pats the rubber-jawed swivel-headed
wringer, slides the galvanized tubs
on a rattling rack, fills washer and tubs
with scalding water, adds home-made soap,

stops to take a breath.
She is young, hair in braids, tie-dye shirt,

sorts piles onto the cement floor,
the lightest go first, those that can take
the heat, then colored clothes, jeans, gardening pants.
a greasy pile from the day
they worked on the car,

puts the whites into the washer,
pulls the lever for the agitator,
ka-chunk swish, ka-chunk swish.
She waits, makes a cup of herbal tea,

pulls up from the hot water, a corner
of a sheet, inserts it between the rollers,
suds squishing out, sheet squashed flat.
Each piece is fed to the wringer
who coughs it up into the first rinse.

She turns the wringer which becomes the sluiceway
to the second tub, carefully repeats, mindful
not to get her braid caught in the wringer.
Last pass through into the basket, first load
squeaky clean, and such a righteous
use of water and energy!

Up the stairs and out to the clothesline,
she is glad her basket is real wicker,
not supermarket plastic,

peeks into the end of the clothesline pole
to see the little brown birds nesting there.

The clothes dry stiff rather than soft,
smelling of fresh air, bleached by the sun.

Her back is already starting to ache.
She sips a little tea and heads back
down the basement stairs.

Highway 12 Time

Remember when we hit the icy patch
on the highway on our way home from
Thanksgiving, me pregnant, our little
son in the back seat. You touched the
brakes. We slid   side to side.

                    Time stopped.

The big red car became a lumbering creature,
peering into the ditch at the left side of the road,
skittering across to stare into the right side,
hovering, sliding until time began again
and we plunged off the road into the snow.

In Butte We Danced

In Butte, we danced, a fabled city,
immigrants from all over the world
came to work in the copper mines,
eating pasties, sarma, povatica,
dancing kolos, horas, polkas and reels.

At the farmers' market in autumn sunshine,
we danced, on the same streets where union men
had marched fourteen thousand strong in overcoats
and fedoras, wanting fair pay for working underground.

Where did you learn to dance like that?
the old Serbian man asked with tears in his eyes.

We laughed as we danced the polka
down the aisle of the famed M&M Cigar Store,
our kids sitting on high stools, drinking Cokes,
where miners once ordered growlers, Sean O'Farrells
even during Prohibition.

After the St. Patrick's Day parade,
half the town crowded into the Silver Dollar bar.
We danced jigs and reels in the midst
of the crowd that showered us
with tightly-folded wads of dollar bills.

Where are you folks from?

The Mai Wah Society honors Chinatown.
Short and loud, the New Year's parade invited us
to follow the Dragon. We walked through the snow,
twirling paper fans, amidst ten thousand firecrackers.

Sunday evenings, we climbed the narrow stairs
to the fourth-floor ballroom of the French chateau
William Clark, Copper King, built for his son.
During breaks in dance practice, we looked out
over the city that made Clark's fortune,
with its head frames and slag piles.

We put on ethnic costumes to go to the Serbian Church
for Yugoslavian Dinner. We danced old-country kolos.
People from the kitchen drummed on pots and pans.
A few joined in the dance.

Superfund Site

One hundred women danced the Cool Water Hula
on the lip of the Berkeley Pit.
Each wrapped two yards of blue fabric around her waist
remembering the year before
when migrating snow geese died after landing
on the toxic water of the open-pit mine.

Before us, the Berkeley's copper-colored water,
on our right, the sickly yellow mine tailings,
behind us, the Granite Mountain Memorial
where 168 miners died underground.

Elegy

Ten thousand snow geese landed on the acidic,
metal laden water of the Berkeley Pit
in Butte Montana on November 28, 2016.
At least three thousand perished.
—Montana Public Radio News

Sorrow
settled
on toxic water
as white geese
spread their wings
across the dark surface

drank deeply
then fell silent
bodies pushed shoreward
by the wind.

Imperial Colleagues Keep Us Up Late

Each November, a festive meeting
of Butte-Anaconda music teachers
in Madame Folland's parlor at 8:30 p.m.
Two grand pianos, maroon velvet drapes,
She in creamy silk and rhinestone glasses.

We were new teachers, our husbands worked
for the Power Company, our offspring
in grade school. We wore jeans and home-made shirts
even when teaching, but that evening
I was in costume in wool pants
and new velour shirt, my hair curled,
dressed up for an uneasy evening.

Top student, Meghan, played twenty minutes
of classics by heart, a last run-through
before the upcoming state auditions,
won by Madame's pupils every year.
Each year's students sounded alike,
crisp and sparkly, the Madam sound.

Applause and lavish praise all around, then
President, Mrs. LaVelle, took charge,
planning recitals, who will bring treats,
who, with a pointed look at new members,
would volunteer to clean up. We
looked away, already exhausted.

Agenda cut short by announcement
that dinner was ready. 10 p.m.
Chicken à la king on puff pastry,
pea salad, a light lemon cheesecake
on fine china, with tea.

The long carpool home, three new teachers
yawning like siblings in the back seat
of Mrs. Kenck's Buick, arriving
before midnight with stories to tell
sleepy spouses of these newfound colleagues,
breaking off to catch a few hours sleep
before the kids woke for breakfast at 6 a.m.

Timeless Doyenne of the Piano

I'm still a knock-out in black and white,
our Madame Folland proclaimed
to the piano teachers the year she turned seventy-five,
her talent and taste said to be a cut above her rivals.

Darling, old age is hell, she said at age eighty,
easing onto a bench outside the concert hall
during intermission, drawing her white fur
around her narrow back.

Still teaching two afternoons a week,
not sure if I am a colleague or a former student.
Music moves forward from opening note to final chord
carrying its servants in relentless arms.

How a Long-Planned Gift Made its Way to the Second Floor Apartment

It arrived in Uptown Butte on an early spring
morning in a carpeted showroom trailer
pulled by a respectable old pickup.
The woman, the wife, in the driver's seat;
beside her. the man, the tuner, with the
unfocused face of one who cannot see.

Quietly they approached the apartment, arm
in arm, setting up the job. How far
the gate? How wide? Steps up to the porch?
The piano was skillfully slid
onto a dolly, a tight fit through the gate.

The buyer, Ukrainian Tamilla
with the bearing and steely strength
of a ballerina, stood ready to throw
her weight into the ascent.

The blind man knew that it would take all his
skill and strength to get the piano up the steep
stairs to the second floor apartment.

He climbed the first flight of the narrow
staircase, counting. At the landing, extended
his arms into his darkness measuring how
high the bannister, how wide the corner,
how high the ceiling? His fingers felt each of the

critical dimensions the waiting piano
would need to turn for the second flight.
No need to ask his sighted wife.
The blueprint of the problem, the strength required was
as clear to him as though he could see.

You need more help. Tamilla knocked
on a neighbor's door and roused a large
sleepy man. She called to her
pale, older son who was watching nearby.

The tuner pushed, lifted the piano from
below, joined by the impetuous Tamilla, the
gentle wife, the reluctant neighbor, the
ineffectual son. The piano reached the
landing, helpers stranded below.

Then the hard part. He must lift the piano
chest-high to clear the bannisters for the turn.

Tamilla picked up her phone. A wiry
neighbor ran across the street. He squeezed
by the others onto the landing, ducked by the
corner of the piano, then claimed the guiding
spot on the upper stairs.

The tuner felt his steadying presence but
knew the lifting must be his own. Muscles
straining, face grimacing, sweat pouring on
that cool spring morning. First

an engineer, then a weight lifter, with
profound dignity, a triumphant roar, he lifted,
he turned.

The piano settled onto the upper flight and
ascended to its new home.

In the tiny living room, he calmly sat down
and played the instrument for an admiring
audience, a professional salesman showing
off his wares.

Tamilla smiled, knowing that her younger
son, the handsome teen
who yearned to play the music
of his barely-remembered homeland, would
think this the finest of birthday gifts.

The Common Song

A choir, a flock of voices,
the low alto enters
for the joy of hearing her
melody slip between
soprano and tenor,
breathing as one
losing herself, finding herself
in the common song.

A tree dark with black birds,
stamped against the flat gray sky.
They lift suddenly, bursting
into the air, one flock swirling,
landing in a nearby tree,
an aerial glissando.

In the shallow water,
a school of minnows, dark
against the sandy bottom,
explore in a fluid dance.
They rise, flowing toward the surface,
reflecting the light. Silver, gold, shine
in joyous counterpoint with the sun.

A buzzing swarm of bees
moves across the darkening field
a murmuring chorus, harmonizing
the same tune. Tendrils of golden
insects lag behind, shoot ahead,
keeping sight of the queen leading
them to a sturdy bush, still humming.

Enemy Fire

the smoke is suffocating,
the sun a hanging red plum,
the moon an old copper coin.

enemy fire has broken out
in the mountains
surrounding the city.
roads are closed, fighters
are the only ones through.

confined to the house,
we feel besieged, depressed.
word has come our friend's son
died by his own hand.
choppers, planes fly over.

like asylum seekers everywhere
we wait.

Late September at the Lake

Clouds fly beneath a dying moon.
The surf roars and splashes,
pines breathe a voiceless *ah*.
I must sit here a little longer.

As the sun rises, waves crash
against the rocks and run along
the shore like frenzied animals.

The wind is cold but I want to hold
onto this moment, at least
until my coffee cup is empty.

Beneath the pines, golden shrubs glow.
Autumn moves leaf by leaf
toward darkness and winter snow.

Avalanche Trail a Few Days after October Wind Storm

Where would you find
shelter from a wind
that tossed and toppled
these massive cedars?

Dark hollow trunks,
root systems torn
from the ground,
standing on edge,
a rose window
in a forest temple.

An ouzel with feet
on the gravel bed
of the stream,
dipped and bobbed,
body blending
with chill dark rock.

New benches
by the receding lake,
mountains white-capped,
back-country smoke
still in the air.

Tiny chipmunk
startled me, darting up
my denim leg,
enticed by crumbs.

Sardines straight from the can,
friends teased,
bears can smell fish
a mile away.

A perfect day
over too soon,
Winter watching
from the mountaintops.

Snowbound

It had been snowing all day
when we arrived home late Friday.

Saturday, the metal table on the deck
where we ate last summer's smores
was covered with a thick layer of white
marshmallow fluff, ready for chocolate,
a graham cracker, a hungry kid.

Sunday, the table was like a tall
loaf of white bread, rising,
ready for the oven, to feed
the hungriest of shoveling men.

Monday, our parked car
was covered with a lofty down comforter
in a parking lot full of puffy white
cartoon cars. It was still snowing.

To free the car we waded into the fluff,
up to our thighs, boots stuck to the ground,
legs pushing wearily through the dough,
scraping holes in the blanket to find
a small blue car, a mere bump
in the ever-deepening snow.

Below Zero

Cold slips through the walls
of the sturdy old house,
like a nocturnal thief,

into closets and cupboards,

settling into the rocker
by the wide window
overlooking the frosty valley,

then
skulking away,

pushed into corner hideouts
by the hulking old furnace
grumbling, growling,
firing up at four a.m.

Winter Is a Time of Waiting

Catkins of frost
hang from barren trees,
fresh snow below,
white sky above.
Broken brush strokes
define black trunk and limb.

A simple landscape
of white
        on white
                on white,
awaiting the sun,
eager to sparkle

against a sapphire sky
for one breathtaking moment,

before the frost falls
like fragile fruit
onto the waiting snow.

Dear Mom,

I've been seeing you
everywhere,
in my friend's profile
as she watched a movie,
in a dream,
on the old back porch,
clear eyes, voice assured.

I remember
how you would laugh,
so many ways,
quietly, mouth closed,
eyes sparkling
giggling like a girl
as we sang
that silly song,
a full blown hoot
as you butchered
a name on the
Grange roll call.

Wisecracking through an
improvised cooking show
filmed by your young
granddaughter,
playing your kazoo
with the kitchen band,

stealing the show
in the only play
you were ever in.

Your joy slipped away
with the years,
as we, your daughters, left.

You thought I would marry
a Philadelphia lawyer.
You were sure I would never
come home to see my parents.

But I didn't and I did,
and the day you looked
at grown-up me
across the dining table
and said appreciatively,
"You're really funny!"
is what I remember.

On the Train after Thanksgiving

To paint that early morning landscape,
begin with a soft wash of misty gray.
add hazy trees in a deeper hue,
brush in a foreground of dark pines.

I saw behind the family façade,
how they hurt each other.
Once hoping for happiness, they are
blown apart by winds of scorn and mistrust.
two minds like the morning clouds,
one layer blowing east, the other west.

Fresh snow covers the passing landscape
in rows of stubble and wheel ruts, cattle
in dark relief. The complexity
of landscape is revealed by the snow.
The sky breaks into layers of yellow, gray, and white.

The Brown Mouse

What was that network of trenches
in the mud and dried grass,
revealed as the last snow melted
in the front yard?

Remembering the brown mouse
running down the sidewalk last fall,
we now think he celebrated
a tiny Thanksgiving,
a cozy Christmas,
just a few feet from our front door

in a borough of one,
a maze of streets and alleys,
excavated like an ancient ruin
by the melting of the snow.

Did he waken in the night,
his mouse-brain driving him
to scamper along his paths,
worrying where he would live
when the snow was gone?

Now his cover is blown,
his private realm open
to eagle, hawk, and me,
and he in exile somewhere,

perhaps in my flower bed,
in the little heap
of mulch and leaves,
beside the columbine.

Our Second Spring

This, our second spring in the Flathead,
the grass is greening,
the maple trees are flowering.
I do not worry that they have bloomed too soon.

I watch for the tiny violets of last year,
the plants my new friends gave me sprout,
familiar now, in the shady beds under the trees.

Our next door neighbor leaves her blinds up.
The bicycle man with the two red dogs
smiles as he rides by.

March 31

March came in like a lion, yes!
Snowy, windy, biting cold,
stalking, snarling, growling.

But to declare today a lamb,
the essence of spring,
clean, white, fresh,
frolicking on green hillsides,
I'd say no.

I wandered out today,
past former mountains of snow
by driveways and parking lots, now
dirty creatures sprawled in the sun.

Days warm just above frost,
nights cool just below. The pace of thaw is
like the steady regard of the shaggy bovine
in the pasture near my home.

March, in like a lion,
Out like a . . .
cow.

Camping Trip

yes

following us wherever we go,
an oversized marshmallow on wheels.

we play house like kids
making do with a pan and a coffee pot,
cup, bowl and spoon.

stand outdoors,
faces to the stars,
long invisible
since my move to town
a half century ago.

sleep with all the windows open,
breezes teasing over
my old honeymoon sleeping bag.

in the morning sip strong perked coffee,
eat instant oatmeal,
slouched into a canvas chair
feet on the picnic table,
new songbirds every morning.

Forty Miles from Canada

Official signs greeted us:
    no fires,
    no guns,
    no alcohol.
    No camping.

A National Historical Park
with picnic tables, vault toilets
and a singular mistrust.

A sandhill crane stood near
the lonely road to the site,
a single antelope grazed,
the meadowlark unduly cheerful,
the wind cold and steady.

A plaque told of
Nez Perce families
war-weary, bone-cold
in a makeshift camp
north
of the Bear Paw Mountains.

U.S. Cavalry circled silently,
shots shattered the dawn,
men, women, children killed, captured
forty miles from refuge
in Canada.

From where the sun now stands,
Chief Joseph said on that day,
I will fight no more forever.

As the wind picked up,
we uneasily pulled away
from the no parking sign,
ceding to the U.S. Government
our right to camp in this lonely place,
forty miles
from Canada.

A Bird Meditation

Sitting in a circle,
in silence, not moving.
Breathing deeply,
shoulders loosen.
A sigh, a yawn,
waiting
as minds begin to still.

Across the mountains
thousands of migrating snow geese,
chattering like high-strung hens,
are gathered on a lake.
Obeying some subtle alarm, they scatter
like silver leaves in a gust of wind.
Skein by skein they return to the lake,
waiting.

The silence deepens.
Breath becomes shallow,
Minds quiet and expand.
settling,
soaring.

A thousand miles west,
seagulls on tidal sand,
in perfect lines, perfect stillness,
wearing gray and white habits
for evening mass,
looking out to sea,
watching, waiting.

Back in the zendo hall
the bell sounds. The cooing
of a dove drifts in
through the open window.

One Alone

On the edge of the woods
the sun golden with smoke,
I heard voices squabbling, jeering.

A flight of ravens, perched
on dead limbs, two here,
three or four there,

one sitting alone.

A family reunion, an
unkindness of ravens,
a clan where all talk,

but not one will listen.

A sudden outcry, and they
flapped to new branches
the pattern entirely changed.

A tribal pow wow, a plot hatched
by a conspiracy of ravens
against a murder of crows.

As I walked home at dusk
you, little raven, were
alone, weakly calling.

The meeting was over
the congress of ravens
had recessed and flown on

without you.

Community

The small crested bird, kept in a cage
while his wing healed, cried loudly for hours
to his flock.

His calls lost urgency,
faded away like a child falling asleep
after sobbing. He no longer ate
the berries we offered. When he died,
we buried him under our apple tree.

Hummingbird in Durango

We held the tiny jeweled kamikaze
in our hands, window struck as he was
from darting into a sky mirage.

Light as milkweed, dandelion fluff,
unembarrassed by our greedy gaze,
he awoke on your sun-warmed palm,
blinked, then flew, tipsy, into the bush.

Crow Talk

I heard them jeering a half mile away.
Four corvids flop-flapping overhead
spreading out, gathering in
like a third grade class at the zoo.

Why do they jaw at each other so?

Are they flying in for a
        a zoning dispute with ravens
                those bullies think they're so smart!
        a street fight with seagulls
                a sassy bunch of thieves!
        a million-crow protest march?

Lovers are said to bill and coo like doves.
Can a crow in his cocky crow's voice say,
or even dream of saying,

        "Honey, I love you?"

Sky-Watching at Lake McDonald

Summer sun low in the sky,
we headed for the dark sky park,
the narrow beach south of the lake.
A trio of photographers
already there, setting tripods.
The word was out, it was a night
for Northern Lights.

The lake darkened, evening breeze
ruffled the water. Ripples and waves
caught the sunset flame.
As the sun glow dimmed
another light in the north
pulsed and faded. *It's beginning,*
a young man announced from
behind his camera.

New arrivals trailed down
from the parking lot, flashlights in hand.
Sitting in our canvas chairs,
we chatted in the darkness
with people unseen.

Dutch tourists, quiet couples,
a wine-giddy woman laughing,
her tripod was jammed,
sleepy daughter fussing, *let's go home*.

We watched the northern light
grow a little, fade a little.
That's all, nothing more, but. . .

Oh! the stars overhead,
layer upon layer
of stars slowly revealed
bright above the pines,
the Milky Way
a luminous cloud.
Together we sat
in awe,
drawn up into the
radiant vastness.

Beyond

Listening to Beethoven

grandpa is hard-of-hearing,
doesn't answer
when spoken to,
reads the paper
when children chatter,
stays home
when the family
goes out to eat,

doesn't hear the pickup
on the gravel drive,
the rumble of thunder,
bleats of sheep,
howl of coyote,
song of warbler
and meadowlark.

a silent tide going out,
left him in stillness on the shore.

lonely when his wife
is at church or out with friends,
he opens the dresser drawer,
lifts from under the socks
his Beethoven disk.

Beethoven knew how it was
to be deaf, pounding
his piano into a snarl
of broken strings,
trying to share the music
in his head.

grandpa
feels a closeness,
a kinship with
the deaf composer.

he puts the disk into the machine,
leans back in his recliner,
turns the volume way up.

Tinnitus

The beekeeper lifts the cover
of the hive, peering through the mesh
bee veil, noting with satisfaction
the drawn-out combs, the honey-filled cells,
puffing the straw-filled smoker to calm,

to distract the bees from the imminent
theft of their summer sweet store.
The bee-man pays no attention to the buzzing,
brushes off the stings. The bees toil on.

The buzz in my head continues
day and night, heavy within my ears,
loudest in the midnight of my sleep,
before morning wakens resting flowers.

Let It All Go

She was my piano teacher, my mentor, for years.

To play the piano, darling, you must relax,
practice slow until all tension is gone.
Engage only the muscles that are needed.
No shoulder raising, please, no grimaces,
no tightly curled fingers, body at ease.

When performing, sink into the relaxation,
don't push, invite the music to sing.
Let the weight of your arms do the work,
play within your ability
or a little outside it, take a deep breath,
then let it all go as it will.

Years later I visited her in the nursing home.
She had been reading words of the Buddha.

I am of the nature to grow old.
There is no escaping growing old..
My actions are the ground on which I stand.

Light, fragile, she was resting in that thin gauze
between the familiar world of the living
and the unknown beyond.
If only I could have been with her
as she passed through that waiting portal.

The night our old dog slipped away, I knew
it was my time to share a loved one's death.
Listening in cool moonlight to her labored breath,
stopping and resuming, again stopping,
I thought that cherished pet offered
those final hard breaths for me to learn
how to sit with death, how it is to die.

Darling, this is what we've been practicing for.
Just relax, let it all go, as it will.

Keeping Track

Numbers rise through the roof,
weights, sets, reps.

Trainers with clipboards, therapists with iPads.
Those who prescribe, who measure progress.

Young women, tropical birds in bright plumage,
chatter, laugh about their men, their kids, their bodies,
dramatic complaining, sisterhood of challenge.

Men, training for competition.
Some not so young anymore but
showing off just a little.

Experienced weight lifters
helping the young guys
Hey, I'll spot for you.

Old men, greeting, *It's about time*
you got here. Joking, *I was waiting*
'til you got the machines warmed up.

The injured, tentatively exploring
the boundaries of their pain to see
what territory can be reclaimed.

In the gym, an hour to feel alive,
to know how vulnerable we
are in the midst of our strength,

and how strong we are even
when in pain.

Numbers rise through the roof,
sets, reps, weights.

Loss

The doctor looked directly into my eyes
There is nothing more we can do.

An open lot on the hilltop
Lombardi poplars, regal pine
framed a neighborhood house
with windows that looked out over the valley.

The row of poplars fell first,
cut, stacked, and hauled, a loss that left
the house naked, vulnerable

We felt uneasy, but we adjusted.
more wrinkles and sags,
a pain that didn't go away.

Under an innocent blue sky
I heard a crunching.
A giant excavator had taken a bite
from the back of the house, dropped it
to the ground, crushed, then loaded it
into a waiting truck.

All that day, I heard that good house
being chewed and swallowed, bite by bite,
the grassy park now a field of dust.

Some irregularities in our lab reports
but we can still get out, even hike a little.
We adapted to the change, a new skyline.

At least they saved the tree, we said,
the tall pine planted when the
house was new.

But a week later, white clouds as witness,
I heard a chainsaw,
the tree lopped off chunk by chunk,
heaped up, hauled away.

Bit by bit, bite by bite, chunk by chunk,
knees, eyes, memory
It became my house, my tree, my loss,

There is nothing more we can do.

Seeing Everything

Mom's first visit from the Midwest,
she looked at the snow-covered peaks
a single magpie, magnificent
in black-and-white western tuxedo,
glided by. She murmured in awe,

Now I've seen everything.

My young sister's first visit west,
we drove through the sagebrush prairie.
As she viewed a herd of cows grazing
under a vast irrigator, she exclaimed,

Now I've seen everything,

but that was before she saw
the moose calf in Yellowstone Park.

Solar eclipse day dawned cloudy,
Seventy fast miles from home, sunshine
was already dimming. When
that ominous shadow rushed toward us
across the prairie, we knew
with a deep shiver that we were seeing
something that terrified our ancestors.

Maybe we've seen everything, we breathed.

Since then we have seen Yellowstone Park's
Morning Glory pool when it was sky blue,

the black spires of Old Town in Prague,
the golden beams in a grove of redwoods,

Irish sheep with rainbow brands
bounding down a grassy slope,

a dark red moon grieving over
burning forests of Montana.

Month by month my eyesight dims,
my mind's eye remembers.

Don’t Need It

I wish I had never seen that woman
    killed in the shower in a motel,
never seen good Dr. Jekyll’s face
    morph into evil Mr. Hyde’s,
never seen the hideous Phantom
    lurking beneath the Opera House.

I’m sorry I saw my sister bit
    in the face by a dog she trusted.
To know that our neighbor went to bed with sight
    and woke up blind was too much for me.

Why did the thought strike me as I walked
    alone down the forest road
    that a mountain lion might be
    thinking me easy prey?

Why must I imagine the approaching logging truck
    on the two-lane highway, will veer toward me
    or that I might, bewitched, swerve toward it?

Our old house creaking in the wind,
    footsteps upstairs when I thought I was alone.
    Demons, changelings, stalkers, rapists.

A new horror movie?
    No thanks.

Restless Earth

rivers of air flow
over the planet,
clouds drift downstream.

human migrants desperate
for work, for fertile fields,
footpaths south to north,

east to west, deer trails
to city gardens. coyotes
and cougars follow.

bull trout swim upstream
to cool water, wolverines
and picas climb to snow.

how can cedar, hemlock
and larch survive? trees
walk only in fairy tales,

but a juniper woods is
springing up, across the
valley from beetle-killed pines.

dying here, seeding there,
inching north sixty-two
miles per century,

migrants
on the restless earth.

I'm Glad

I'm glad I never had to pepper spray a bear,
glad I didn't have to live in a house with rats
or work in a copper mine underground.

I'm glad I didn't have to pick pin feathers
from smelly turkeys as my mother did,
glad I didn't inherit her varicose veins.

So glad I didn't have all my teeth pulled
as my dad did or work swing shift in a factory,
coming home, exhausted, to tend his bees.

I'm glad I didn't have to marry an old man
chosen by my mother, or stand at a window
in a burka watching my brother leave for school.

I'm glad I didn't have to trudge hundreds of miles
for asylum, toddler on my back,
or huddle all winter in a refugee camp.

I'm so glad I don't have melanoma,
carcinoma or lymphoma. Deeply glad
I have not wept at my own child's grave.

What I Can Do: An Ode to Our Earth

I was raised on lard, second-hand smoke
and DDT. Car rides with my chain
smoking dad behind the wheel,
Mom spraying the screen door to keep
the flies away, Grandma's fried chicken.

Hapless natural food guru Adele Davis
died of cancer. I'm still here, but
it's too late for me to save my body
by eating organic, shunning smokers,
avoiding pesticides.

To be honest, Great Mother, it's you
I worry about now. Oil spills,
power plant emissions, pesticides.
Like me, you can't escape the blights
that impair your health.

In a few swiftly-passing years
someone fresh and clean will take
my place, but you, you must endure
eon after eon, birthday after smoky birthday,
with far too many thoughtless guests.

I sing to you, Terra Firma, our cradle,
our home. I remember that first time I saw
your picture taken from outer space.
You were gorgeous, with your swirls
of white, your sapphire oceans.

We are searching for a doctor
with expertise in your condition. Don't try
to hide your fevers, your swinging moods.
Let your storms shake us up. Remind us
ever and again that you need our care.

When I eat organic, I do it for you.

The Wind in the Willows 2016
Toad writes a Very Very Special Poem

I am Toad of Toad Hall,
the finest house on the River.
To be honest with you, my friends
Ratty and Mole and even old Badger
are losers. I love them dearly, but
there's no getting around it,
they live in holes in the ground.

They say I got my money
from the Old Toad, but that was just
my start. I've made amazing
investments in boats, motorcars
and real estate. I really know
how to seal a tremendous deal.

The Wild Wood is full of
stoats and weasels, They're
all right in a way, but you can't
trust them. They are not nice,
disgusting really. I put up an
iron fence to keep them out.

I'm number one in every poll
of the River folk. Believe me,
I could steal a motor car,
break out of prison
and still be at the very top!

Ratty says this poem of mine,
is full of narcissism, full of
swagger and swank, that I should
be more genteel, more polite
but to be honest, my friends,
he’s a total loser,
though I do love him dearly.

Liberty Valance Had a Gun

Some insist if we all carried guns
we'd be safer,
It didn't work that way in the wild west,
a Texan remarked.

In the old movie, the city lawyer
in dishwasher's apron stood up
against the gunfighting thug,
Liberty Valance.

Lawyer survived, thanks to his friend
who got off a quick lethal shot,
cutting down that vile gunslinger,

which leads me to think
safety is all about
friendship,

which is where I'd like
this poem to go,

liberating me
from preemptively
packing a pistol
in my purse.

Activism

Loving the theatre as I do,
I nodded yes when asked at the dorm party,
Who wants to learn to do a stage fall?

Falling is like dancing, only more so,
weight on left foot, lean to the right
and let your body crumple
over your hip and toward your leg,
until you unfold and are lying
at ease on your right side.

In long-ago concert halls delicate
ladies in narrow corsets fainted
when music brimmed with passion.
Hmm. That gave me an idea

to go to a political rally,
to hear the speaker say something
untrue with a smug surety.
I would abruptly stand, cry *no!*
a thousand times no!
in a great impassioned voice
and collapse to the floor.

As kind souls knelt to offer
first aid, the speaker would
stand helpless, his message
forgotten.

Later I would quietly slip out and at home
I would ruminate on fainting goats,
whole herds of whom would topple
to the ground when startled.

Free or Not Free

I hadn't really thought it through
when I dropped my name into the box.
Weeks later the letter came. *You have won!*
Twenty-five dollars worth of dahlias, free.

Now I have the responsibility
for these dry little tubers
with names like race horses:

> Glen Echo,
> Brookside Cherry,
> Dandie Alexi,
> Falcon Future, and
> even I'm a Hottie.

Arthritic backs laid railroad ties for a sunny bed.
Strong college boys were hired to move the dirt.
Tired arms pounded stakes into the hard ground.
Aching legs crawled down the rows
as cold hands placed each tuber, carefully,
lovingly, uncertainly but with a gentle pat.

Then wait. A long time.
Though named like race horses,
these little bits of life were in no hurry.
Each emerged, greeted with more compost.
A bud or two appeared and finally a flower,
butter yellow with delicate pink edges.

Beautiful! But,
a deer ate it.

We bought a motion-triggered sprinkler
to chitter wetly at hoofed intruder.

Each day a fiesta of yellow and orange, a riot of red,
the soft pink of a lover's bouquet.

Too soon, an early frost.
Now vases of flowers all over the house.
The dahlias weren't free,

but now I am.

Winter Is Like That

We have never been old before.
Too tired was not an option for us,
but now this winter, it is time to rest.
Winter is the ancient refuge of the weary.

Short days inspire us to live as free
as any creature of field or forest,
without cold drizzles of duty hanging over.

In the ageless mountains of Montana
with spring biding its time, we wait for north winds
to sheath their icy blades, wait until it's safe
to emerge from beneath the snow into the light.

Winter Villanelle

No matter what she does, she's always cold,
the fog presses close this time of year.
Again she sits and waits, her breath grows slow.

The house is hidden by the blowing snow,
she longs for daylight like a star-blind deer.
No matter what she does, she's always cold.

The chill reminder that she has grown old,
the piercing truth she doesn't want to hear.
Again she sits and waits, her breath grows slow.

Craving light, she lingers on the threshold,
still possessed by that age-old fear.
No matter what she does, she's always cold.

Long nights sit blind upon her sevenfold;
dreams lie down upon a funeral bier.
Again she sits and waits, her breath grows slow.

Against all pity she stands resigned but bold,
to dare the fog to lift and all things clear.
No matter what she does, she's always cold.
Again she sits and waits, breath deep and slow.

Crabby Like Me

It's been raining all day.
I have a cold.
Nancy Pelosi is on the radio.
She sounds crabby
like me.

To lie down is to cough,
so I sit and look
at the sky, rust-tarnished gray, graywater pink.
Sullen, crabby
like me.

It's been raining all week.
I have a cold.
The doctor says the cough may last a month. Then
it will be Spring.
I'll see

the Sun.
Maybe.

The Irish Know How to Live with Rain

It was raining, had been raining
most of our week in Ireland. Clutching
our umbrellas, we trudged through puddles
past the small deserted park.

A cuppa tea would be nice, I proposed.
From the tea-room window, we saw the sun
ease through the blanket of clouds,
the park filling with those who had waited
long to feel the sun on their faces.

Young men stood smoking and chatting
where moments earlier there were
only quiet paths and empty benches.

Shopkeepers posted "closed" signs on doors,
stepped across the cobbled street,
students streamed from schoolyard gates.

Fresh from daycare, toddlers waddled
free with balloon strings tied
around their wrists, squealing their joy.

The lawn was as green as June rain,
the longed-for sun as golden as dreams.

On a dried-off bench, we lunched
on sandwiches pulled from our pockets.

Beautiful Moon, Super Moon
January 31, 2018

We call you
rose moon,
snow moon,
wolf moon and
hunter's moon.

You are our companion, the beacon
we rely on for serenity,
for the wisdom to know

reflected light can be
as perfect and as fair
as light created from within.

When you are as near and bright
as you were last night,
you shine infinity back to us.

Aurora Borealis

Behind the trees
green auroras dance
all night,
leaping, falling.

A veil lifted,
thin space revealed,
spirit dancers
cast elongated
green shadows,
calling
the newly free

to join in the dance
behind the pines
that begins
some evenings
around midnight,
leaps and falls
until dawn.

"Buffalo Robe for Sale"

The seller was an Indian woman,
drums, blankets, feathers, beadwork filled
her small home on Butte's flats.
You, O hide of bison, displayed on the wall,
I liked your woolliness, your size,
large enough to warm two campers
on a cold night in a tent.

After the slaughter of millions
of your noble kin, a surviving band
was sold to Charles Conrad
to graze on his land west of town.
Time after time, they moved
to the open hillside to the north.
Settlers called it the Buffalo Hill.

Hagel Custom Tanning, Kalispell
stamped on your hide. We mused you might be
from the Conrad Buffalo Herd,
one of the young, whose grandmothers
chose this hill that drew the herd
so insistently that Mr. Conrad
let them have their way.

Deciding where to live out our lives,
we felt a push, a nudging
toward the Flathead Valley.
Our realtor showed us homes
across the area. Like you,
the one we were drawn to
was on that open knoll north of town.

We brought you home to the Buffalo Hill
where your ancestors found refuge.
You are lying under our
grand piano soaking up
overtones and spring sunshine
dappled by the tall trees
outside the window.

The Hospital Pianist

She walked quietly into the deserted lobby,
lifted the lid of the piano, pulled out
the bench, adjusted the music rack,
opened a thick notebook. Brackets, arrows,
numbers in different colors informed the pages.

The music was a full-length recital
She felt nervous as though there was
an audience sitting in rows before her,
rather than the empty couches and
hurrying doctors.

The Bach chorale was first, bringing serenity
to herself and to the ears in the sickrooms,
an introduction, a warm-up, a prayer
floating down the corridors.

Beethoven's Op. 110 Sonata
full of light, transcendence. The whispery
transitions worried her so early
in the program, but she was pleased
with the looping butterflies of sound.

She had played Mozart's B minor Adagio
for a friend's funeral, grieving, then as now,
stretching the time as the last measures shifted
to the major key bringing solace.

Playing Chopin and Brahms, she caressed
the keys. The patients, the nurses, remembered,
first loves, lost loves from those days long ago
when everything seemed possible.

Rachmaninoff's prelude offered sleigh bells,
church bells, brooding basses, a Russian
love affair set in a time when steam rose
from hot pools and snowflakes lay on a lover's hair.

Debussy, a sigh of summer, floating
on quiet water, escape from darkness
of winter, of aging, of loss.

Finally Bartok. a dance in pounding
Bulgarian rhythm with dissonance
to spare. She had been advised that pleasant
music was best for the hospital,
but she knew the patients would understand
if anyone can
that life is both consonance and dissonance.

She looked around the lobby. A woman
folding a lunch bag smiled and said *thank you.*
She nodded in return and closed her book.

And walked out into the waning light.

On the Path: A Road Trip

Speed limit signs advise
take it easy and *what's your hurry?*

I've been on this trip for years.
It's unclear where I am going
but staying on the road, I know I am not lost.

When unable to see the lines ahead
from mist, or snow, or confusion,
I keep going, one wheel on the rumble strip.

Frequently stopping to breathe deeply,
I consult the roadmap in my head.
You are here, right here, right now.

I drive on with more confidence.
I've thrown out a few of the bags
carefully packed before I set out.
The car feels lighter, yet more stable.

I drive on, singing.

Retreat Reflections

Friday Morning By The Lake

Alone I sit on a rock by the lake,
silver, flat, muted like me.
a strange cry from behind the cabins,
a dark wide-winged bird flies over.

Breakers rise and fall as the minutes pass,
Wavelets break against a protruding rock
like small animals racing by
in a trail of white spray.

The shoreline stones are transformed
to rich colors as the water touches them.
My fingers find the edge of the cold water.

Saturday Morning Dreaming in Two Worlds

At this early dawn meditation,
my head feels unbearably heavy.
I take a deep breath and . . .

for a moment I am at home
in the kitchen, with you, my love.
You are frying ham; it sizzles enticingly.
You turn, happy to see me.

Breathing out, I am back
at the retreat, wide awake,
my heart warmed by the breath of home,
my mind open to the mystery of all that is.

yes

Retreat at the Monastery

The temple bell before dawn,
crescent moon hanging low,
being up at five a.m., a quiet joy.

Hundreds of shoes heaped by the door,
Ocean of Peace meditation hall.
A wooden folding chair my hard seat.

The tiny nun, impossibly old,
slumped on my shoulder as she dozed.
Her smile of apology so sweet.

Brown-robed monks and nuns cooked meals,
greens in fragrant broth with rice noodles.
Bright koi drifted in the pond nearby.

Time for red manzanita, white sage on the hills,
for knowing the sacred in every rock and tree,
time to breathe like a buddha by a bodhi tree.

A Quilt of Stones

The bleak high-plains cemetery
on the hilltop outside of town,
local family graves clustered
toward the far end of the drive,

remains of funeral ribbon
and wind-flattened plastic flowers
against the east fence.

On a side plot, two graves,
a navy man beside a woman
born decades before,
a mosaic of stones,
pressed into cement,
quartz, granite
sandstone and glass.

Someone who cared, maybe this son,
sat for long hours, choosing,
arranging stones, remembering
his mother's life.

The name was Plunkett,
no one seems to know the family.
Perhaps just passing through,
so we called the decorated plot
the gypsy quilt.

Just yesterday I learned
that my eighth-great-grandmother
was an "Indian Maiden"
of the Wampanoag Tribe
of Massachusetts, married
to an Englishman in 1649.

That tiny added stone
colors my life quilt in brighter hues,
my story more connected to the Earth,
to the People who came before.
Even though I, like the Plunketts,
am just passing through.

Daughters of an Unhappy Mother

live in dark forest huts outside a walled town,
send hopeful envoys to the gateway each morning.
The doorkeeper says with a frown of rebuke
Go away. We feel punk. We can't see you today.

They return feeling guilty to friends and to sisters,
learn to play dirges, sing sad songs in parts,
read long-winded tales about happier people
and self-help books to comfort their hearts.

Every so often the gate will be open
the gatekeeper greets them with hugs and with smiles.
there is laughter and feasting and dancing in kitchens
and stories of all things gone wrong and gone right.

Little by little, they learn to see branches
emerge from darkness with the coming of dawn,
learn to accept the city with kindness,
learn to be happy most of the time.

Yes

On the Day My Sister Died

I did ordinary things.
My friend brought pears. I washed the sheets.
The trees were fountains of gold and red.

I should have known she would go first. Curious,
she pushed all the buttons, pulled all the levers
while I stood back, careful, cautious.

My duet partner, she was Rose Red
to my Snow White, a musical ball of fire.
Her energy carried both of us in piano and song.

We kicked, cried and blamed our way through childhood,
this sister and I.
Bareback we rode double, singing with the horse's gait,
fell out of trees, suffered bee stings, measles, chicken pox.

It has been seven years since the family met
at my new house. Cathy brought kazoos
jacks and joy to our last time together.

Why is this happening? The cancer
moved quickly, resisting miracles,
stealing hearing, bringing delirium.

I missed the train home. She gathered
run-away thoughts for our last phone call.
Have you been there long, she sighed.

I've been sick but I'm coming,
I love you she murmured,
love you, love you, drifting away.

Her son's quiet voice across the continent
separating us for years, invited me on this day
to say goodbye to Cathy, as she slept.

She will be buried near our parents' plots,
in the leafy cemetery of our hometown.
Sister of mine, rest in peace.

Grandmothers

Grandma Gladys had an upturned mind,
talked in a good-natured scholarly way
about topics with lots of details.
Her God was a reasonable Protestant,
who respected his Church, even the
Church Secretaries. She lived in an
orderly world, though she kept house
like a bachelor. They ate plain food,
broccoli, sitting at a corner of the table
beside a stack of papers. Ideas swirled
in her head, sometimes she noticed her
family, listened, laughed. Her old farmer
husband, silent, got on her nerves.

Grandma Mabel grumbled that life
had not been fair to her. She was not
searching for God, but for love, the
divorce was her sorrow. She had been
the meticulous housekeeper for a banking
family in the city and knew how things
should be done. She baked desserts,
full of lard and love, chicken with crispy
skins. Planted fertile vegetable gardens
in straight rows, zinnias and cosmos,
watched Cubs baseball, boxing, and
Lawrence Welk on TV. Every month
"True Romance" came in the mail.

When my house is clean
and filled with color, I feel Grandma
Mabel within me. When I sit
scowling at the computer,
looking for the right word,
it’s Grandma Gladys. Impatient
with my husband? Grandma Gladys.
Savoring a slice of apple pie,
tangy, sweet with flaky crust?
Of course, it must be Grandma Mabel.

yes

John Wetz's Funeral

On the autumn afternoon that the engine
of my Dad's body coasted to a halt,
a hospice nurse sat quietly nearby.
He was surprised by death. *Do you realize*
I could die? he had asked in his 94th year.

His mechanic's hands were without grease;
his reading glasses on his nose, a slight smile
on his lips as he lay in a steel-blue casket,
amid glowing flowers in the honeyed tones
that his bees had once coveted.

The Grange is meeting Upstairs, said one
of the young men who called him "Dad,"
after their own fathers were gone, looking
at the Grange chapter photo of 50 years ago.

The son-in-law read Psalms and Proverbs
in ringing tones. The daughters remembered
their father standing alone in the yard,
watching a violent thunderstorm directly overhead,
while they huddled indoors with their mother.

The sisters sang in three parts as they often did.
The congregation smiled as they reminisced about

Wetz, the hayfield fire fighter,
Wetz, the mechanic who could fix anything
with the odds and ends scattered about his shop,
Wetz, the expert on almost any topic.

The benediction

A steam whistle, the heavy chugging
of an accelerating engine.
The steam club members looked around, puzzled.
The daughters jumped to their feet and clapped,
as the casket was rolled rapidly down the aisle.

The organist, grandson of a Granger,
segued from a pounding steam engine effect
into a jubilant postlude.

John Wetz would have laughed.

In the last years of his life, John Wetz was
building a steam-powered automobile.

yes

Christmas Morning

I want to tell you that Dog
woke me at midnight,
licked my dreaming face,
said *Come, my love*.

I want to tell you we
opened the window to frosty air,
that in the yard below, a shuffle
of wings, a far-off song.

I want to tell you that Owl,
perched on the rail, said *look, look*
and there was the star shining
through the parted clouds,

and Dog said God Himself was abroad
striding through the darkness south of town,
and he asked *now do you believe*
we animals speak in your tongue on Christmas Eve?

But, of course, Dog, more gifted in love
than in truth, has misled me before,
and so I am not sure now in morning light
if he spoke or what he said.

Expedition on Christmas Afternoon

They had looked forward to being together for so long,
but now, after the gifts and all, they were restless.

Let's go for a walk, someone said.
I'll pack some provisions, said someone else,
stuffing her pockets with candy.
They each assumed a name, a persona.

The Eskimo was dressed in fur, the Dwarf in pink fleece,
the Abominable Snowman wore cool blue down.
Grandma Bigfoot was authoritative in red boots.

They set forth into fantasy land, squinting
into the sunlight to see the frozen pond ahead.
Bigfoot decided quickly; their way lay to the left,
between the frosty shore and the massive huts of the
natives.

Their confidence grew, as they marched along
in the bitter cold, until they reached the far shore where
howls and barks of unseen wolves chilled their valor.
Cautioned not to run, the expedition tiptoed by,
imaginary bows at the ready.

The landscape was deserted but for a sinister gang
of natives out on the lake, swinging sticks
at bones that skittered across the ice.

As they rounded the lake toward home,
the morale of the expedition unexpectedly plummeted.

The Eskimo and Dwarf burst out running down the hill,
a full-blown insurrection despite orders to stop.
The Nameless Enemy cruised by in a black hearse,
The party crouched, regrouped and hurried toward home.

They sat down, faces rosy, beside the Christmas Tree
to eat their provisions and chronicle their adventures,

together at that one hour on that one winter day
when such make-believe was still possible.

Car Keys

I took a deep breath as I dropped the keys
into the top drawer of the bureau,
knowing even then
I would never again use them.

Sixty years ago my dad eagerly
taught me to drive. Parenthood
and joy in all things mechanical
had finally come together.

We started and stopped the old Ford Falcon
in the oat field stubble out back,
mastering the coordination
of gas and gear, clutch and brake

until I could set off without killing the engine,
ready for the gravel road, other cars,
shifting up into higher gears,
higher speeds.Then my mom weighed in.

Take the back roads; don't drive over
fifty miles an hour, slow down on gravel.
You never know what the other guy
will do or what will fail on our old car.

If I still lived in the gravel-grid Midwest,
where I could tool along at Mom-speed,
I would keep those keys. My one slow eye
would be enough to see me through.

Did I ever tell you that I'm good with men?
that I chose a man who is a lover in
ways that I never expected,
a man who says to me every day,
I'll take you anywhere you want to go.

About the Author

Generations of my family farmed in northern Illinois, but I longed for a life of music and for the magic of mountains outside my window, and so I became a Montana piano teacher. When I could no longer see the sharps and the naturals, the lines and the spaces, I retired. A year later, I began writing poetry at Flathead Valley Community College.

The poems were written, one each week, for the Poetry Workshop class. I was pleased to see as I began thinking of this book that they tell my story in a more authentic voice than I could otherwise have found.

Acknowledgements

Previous versions of poems in this collection first appeared in the following publications:

"First Dance," "Winter Villanelle," and **"Snowbound"** were first printed in *Poems Across the Big Sky II*, 2016.

"Fireflies" was first printed in *As It Happens, FVCC Academic Journal,* Spring 2016.

"Hop In" was first printed in *Whitefish Review*, #22, Summer/Fall 2018.

"What I Can Do: An Ode to Our Earth" was first printed in *Whitefish Review*, #23, Spring/Summer/Fall 2019